EARL
THE GRUMP

EBURY
PRESS

1 3 5 7 9 10 8 6 4 2

Ebury Press, an imprint of Ebury Publishing
20 Vauxhall Bridge Road
London SW1V 2SA

Ebury Press is part of the Penguin Random House
group of companies whose addresses can be found
at global.penguinrandomhouse.com

Penguin
Random House
UK

First published by Ebury Press in 2016

Special thanks to Jon Swan, Derek Bloomfield and
Christie Bailey

Stock images © Shutterstock and photographs on
page 12, 62 and 63 © Getty images

www.eburypublishing.co.uk

A CIP catalogue record for this book is
available from the British Library

ISBN 9781785034091

Printed and bound in China by Toppan Leefung

EARL
THE GRUMP

IF EVERY DOG HAS ITS DAY,
THEN WHERE THE HELL IS MINE?

@earlthegrump

MY NAME IS EARL

I'm a dog. I am not your pal. I am not
loyal. I am not your cutie-wootie-pie.
I'm none of these things. I will tell
you what I am, though. I am grumpy.
In fact, I'm always grumpy. And I am
hungry. Which is making me even more
grumpy. Got any food for me? Peanut
butter, if possible. No? Sigh. Typical.
So what are you doing here then?

I have a feeling you've picked this book
up for guidance and advice. You might
have some problems, or need some counsel.
You might be thinking, What would Earl
do?

Let's get one thing straight. I don't
care about your problems. So you can
do whatever. Here's an idea! Let's turn
this whole thing around. Instead of you
wondering what good old Earl can do for
you, how about you think about what you
can do for me? How about that? What about
me? I never asked to be the internet's
grumpiest canine. It just happened
that way.

But, while you're here, I'll tell you
what you can do. You can buy this book.
The £8.99 you spend may momentarily make
my world a better place, although knowing
my luck I wouldn't bet on it. But, even
if it did, I wouldn't give a damn anyway.
But give it a try. It's the least you can
do to make yourself feel better about
your pathetic existence.

Now go away and never bother me again.

Earl (the dog)

FORGET IT

NOT GONNA HAPPEN

MY INCREDIBLY GRUMPY SO-CALLED LIFE

X

This is where I live. I may be called Earl, but believe me, this is no castle. The grass is pretty rough to sit on too and stinks of imposturous cats.

I spend a lot of time looking outside, seeing what the neighbor's dog is up to, monitoring the cat population and making sure no one pees on my patch.

X

Sometimes I like it outside, sometimes
I don't. Usually tree rats — squirrels to
you — are in my garden. I hate them. Then
I have to avoid the neighbors, the postman,
the dog next door. And you never know when
you might run into a feline enemy. But, you
know, at least I get to see other people
being miserable, especially on a week day
when they're off to work.

Napping is the
only thing in
life that I can
bear, mainly
because I'm
unconscious and
unaware of the
unbelievable
drivel going
on around me.

But even that
gets ruined by
this monstrosity.
Humans are a
bad idea.

The humans that
own me are so
cheap, I have
to scavenge for
peanut butter.
One day I'll own
them and run
my own peanut
butter empire.

At the moment,
I sometimes have
to demean myself
for their
amusement. I'll
get my revenge.

THINGS AREN'T
AS BAD AS THEY SEEM

THEY'RE WORSE

Earl

Earl the grump

Go away. I'm probably sleeping. Leave me a comment, but I might not reply.

Earl's Likes

Jennifer Lawrence

Peanut Butter

Naps

I LIKE DOGS' BUTTS

AND I CANNOT LIE

I LIKE MY MORNINGS LIKE I LIKE MY CATS

IF THEY NEVER CAME AROUND

EARL'S DISLIKES

ENTHUSIASTIC PEOPLE

ARE SUCH HARD WORK

I GOT SO MANY TROUBLES

I HAD TO TELL THEM TO GET IN LINE

I LIKE CATS TOO

LET'S EXCHANGE RECIPES

To: Cat protection society

CC:

Dear Cat protection society

I can't tell you how happy I was to find your organization on the internet. I think it is fantastic that people like you exist. I am writing to you because I need protecting from cats. My daily life is made a misery by felines. Let me give you a few examples:

> they come into my garden on their nasty, catty paws
> they drink from my outside special bowl, leaving it smelling of cat breath. Yuck
> they do unmentionable rancid things and bury it in MY plant pots
> they taunt me through the window when I'm locked indoors
> they worm their way into the affections of the humans who are my property.

There are many other bad and heinous things cats do, but I don't want to come across as a moaner. As you can see, my situation is already pretty dire so please can you start protecting me as soon as possible?

Thanks

Earl (the dog)

You may have seen me on the internet, I'm quite a big deal. ────────────→

NEVER EXPECT ANYTHING

AND YOU WON'T BE DISAPPOINTED

To: Cat protection society

CC:

Dear Cat Protection Society

I was very disappointed to receive your email.
It turns out you actually are in the business
of protecting cats, not people from cats. Let me
tell you, that's not a business anyone needs.
Your name is misleading and I think you should
change it. Here are a few suggestions you
might like to consider to avoid anyone
getting confused in future:

> The down with dogs anti-dog society
> Cats are bad and we are their evil
  henchmen society
> Fishy cat-breath rules society
> We think cats are great and that's because
  we are a mad and deluded association (this is
  my own personal favorite).

However, cross with you as I am, perhaps you
might yet be of some use. As you call yourselves
experts on cats, I would appreciate your
ideas on how I can get rid of them
from my life. Forever.

Earl (the dog)

In case you've forgotten who I am. ——————→

To: Cat protection society

CC: The President of the United States; Jennifer Lawrence; Scooby Doo (c/o Shaggy); Khaleesi from Game of Thrones

Dear Cat protection society,

Well! I didn't expect that! I was only trying to help you out with my suggestions for your new name, but I guess you are over-sensitive and prone to hissy fits. Funny, I know a lot of cats like that.

For your information, I am not 'an example of everything that is wrong with society' as you so suggest. I am a law-abiding citizen, who has never gone into someone else's garden or buried unmentionable things in plant pots. Unlike your clients. In fact, I could have been a guide dog but I failed the agility test because of my short legs. Plus, I'm not in the business of helping others.

Anyway, nor am I an 'animal hater'. For your information I am an animal myself, and have been since birth. I know this because my humans regularly remind me by tying me to a lamppost. Plus, I don't have fingers, which makes opening peanut butter jars quite difficult.

I think your catty attitude towards me stinks, frankly, and I think it's time people knew what you are really like. As you will see, I have copied this email to some very influential people who are also very close friends of mine, and I am also writing to the Leader of the Free World, recommending he take drastic steps to take you down. I look forward to your shady outfit being shut down very soon.

Earl (the dog)

To: President of the United States/
Commander in Chief

CC:

Dear POTUS (I hope you don't mind me calling you this: I saw it on the West Wing and it makes me feel like we're already friends).

How are you? I'm fine.

I am writing to you to warn you that we have a common foe right here in our backyard (literally: I saw two of them in my garden this very morning). Cats! That's right, cats. Time is short, and unless we act now, all might be lost and the Cats Protection underworld will take over.

I have been taking necessary precautions already. Unbeknown to my humans I have made a big hole in the back of the sofa that I can climb into. This is my panic room, and you are welcome to join me in it any time, along with the First Lady and a few staff (if they are very small — it's only a two-seater sofa). I have already laid in supplies to ensure we can hide out for a few weeks. I have peanut butter, meaty treats and a few bones. If you are coming, perhaps you could bring some extra food? I get pretty hungry when I'm stressed, and also when I'm not stressed.

Anyhow, rather than having to hide in the sofa while cats take over the world, wouldn't it be better if you used your powers and just called in the Army now to sort the problem out? Maybe a drone strike or two? We can soon have those cats back in their place and restore proper order. I don't think we need to involve the Navy because cats don't like water.

Earl (the dog)

Some people think I could run for President, but I prefer to remain anonymous, except online — I'm a big deal on there.

THE PROBLEM WITH TROUBLESHOOTING

IS THAT TROUBLE SHOOTS BACK

NOTHING HELPS MY BAD MOOD

LIKE SPREADING IT AROUND

WHEN PEOPLE SAY
'HAVE A NICE DAY'

I TELL THEM
I HAVE OTHER PLANS

HOW TO HAVE A ~~GREAT/GOOD/TOLERABLE/~~ PARTY

I LOVE PARTIES. SEE HOW EXCITED I AM:

X

As your first guest arrives, remember that in fact you HATE parties. And people. Don't smile and make sure not to show any sign of happiness.

Mingle!
Spend time with the trash can to show how little you think of human interaction.

Make sure there is barely any food and drink to make people feel as unwelcome as possible in an effort to force people to leave as quickly as possible.

If you really have to, try to appear interested in your guests' stories, however boring you find them. But mutter under your breath what a waste of time this is... they'll get the message.

The best part of a party is when the last guest leaves. Why did you invite that guy? He's a moron.

NOTE TO SELF. NEVER MAKE THE MISTAKE OF HAVING A PARTY AGAIN.

GIVE A DOG A BONE?

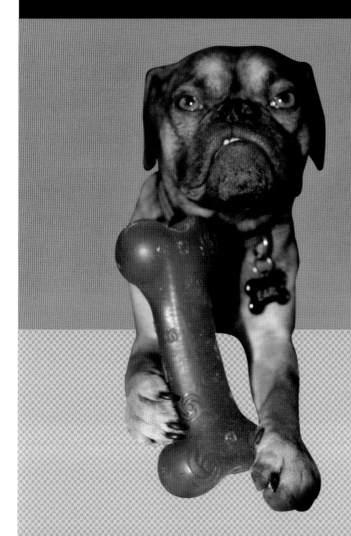

DON'T BOTHER

HOW TO MAKE THE MOST OF THE YEAR, WHATEVER THE SEASON

I SAW A BUTTERFLY ONCE

A BIRD ATE IT

HAVE YOURSELF A MERRY LITTLE

NOTHING

EVERY PATH

HAS A PUDDLE

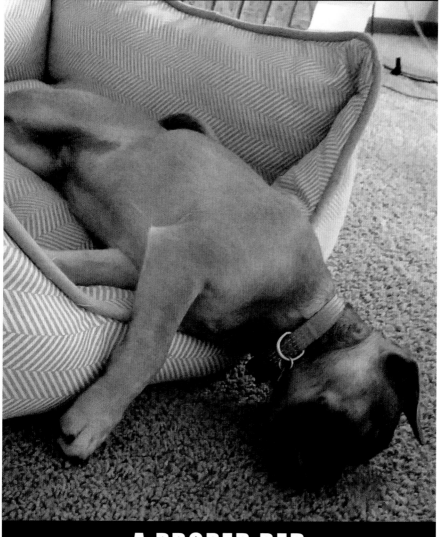

THEY'RE SO CHEAP,
THEY WON'T EVEN BUY ME

A PROPER BED
#EARLSWORLDPROBLEM

I THINK I MUST HAVE MEMORY PROBLEMS

BECAUSE I CAN'T REMEMBER
WHEN I ASKED FOR YOUR OPINION

I SHOWER EVERY DAY

IN MISERY

I TOLD YOU

ALWAYS MAKE SURE THAT PEANUT BUTTER. IS. ON. THE. LIST.

POEM

When will you buy my peanut
butter?

It's making me so mad that I
stutter

The last jar was nicked by the
cats

And the fact that you haven't
replaced it is rats

If you don't sort this soon
you'll feel bleak

When I'm using your wardrobe to
take a leak

WHO'S A GOOD BOY?

BEING GRUMPY

GIVES ME PURPOSE IN LIFE

THINGS THAT HAVE MADE ME GRUMPY TODAY

X

The neighbor and his blinking dog

My nap being disturbed by humans

X

The unavailability of peanut butter-flavor dog food

Cats doing a drive-by hissing at me

MY LIFE IS AWFUL

TODAY I LEARNED A
NEW WORD ON THE INTERNET

MEH!

YOU HEARD ME

SCOOP MY POOP

IF IT'S THE THOUGHT
THAT COUNTS

YOU SHOULDN'T
HAVE BOTHERED

OUT OF HERE

IF THERE WAS SOMEWHERE
BETTER TO GO

YOU CAN BE ANYONE
YOU WANT ONLINE

LOOKS LIKE MOST PEOPLE
CHOOSE TO BE STUPID

EARL'S BLUNDERS OF THE WORLD

too WET

too WONKY

too FRENCH

too POINTY

too COLD

WIN SOME, LOSE SOME

DON'T CARE EITHER WAY

I'M ONLY GRUMPY

ON DAYS THAT END IN Y

WE ARE BORN WET, HUNGRY AND NAKED

THEN THINGS GET WORSE

I'M PRACTISING

NOT GIVING A DAMN

THEY CALL ME...

LONG FACE SILVER

1. Armageddon:
   An asteroid
   threatens
   human
   existence.
   It's supposed
   to be the
   size of
   Texas.
   Winner.

EARL THE GRUMP

ARMAGEDDON

2. UP: First half of the
   film was good. I didn't
   reach the end, the old
   man looked like he was
   going to end up happy.

3. Grumpy Old
   Men: Says
   it all.

GRUMPY OLD MEN

EARL

EARL

EARL

UP

TAIL
WAGGERS

Earl stars in

SCROOGE

4. Scrooge: Christmas is awful.

🦴🦴🦴

5. Groundhog Day: Bill Murray is really grumpy.

🦴🦴🦴

Groundhog Day

TAIL WAGGERS

1. Marley and Me: The dog dies.

2. Turner and Hooch: Begins OK, lots of action and laughs. Then the dog dies.

3. Old Yeller: Heroic dog defends boy from bear and wins boy's heart. Then the dog dies.

Marley & Me

CANINE CATASTROPHE!

4. The Incredible Journey. 3 dogs cross hundreds of miles to find their owners. Don't you get it, guys? They abandoned you! F@*% them!

5. Bolt. This dog had it all: fame, fortune, money. But he gives it up for love. Sap.

CANINE CATASTROPHE!

EARL'S GUIDE TO OTHER DOGS

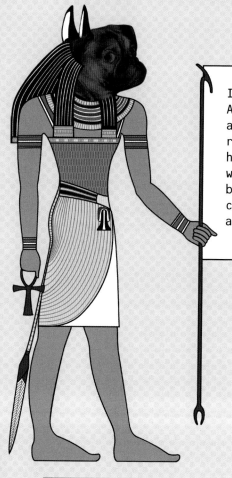

I thought about Anubis. He's a god and a dog. Then I remembered that he has a human body, which is a downside, but he does have a cool stick. I'd make a better god.

Myself and the only other beings on this planet I can actually spend more than 5 minutes around, without wanting to explode.

Laika. The first ever creature in space was a dog, obviously. Then I remembered that I'd make a better space dog.

Pluto. He's the only Disney guy who doesn't wear human clothes, which I can muster a tiny amount of respect for, but he comes across as a positive, obnoxious buffoon. So, have another picture of me.

EARL

Lassie. Lassie was a boy, poor guy always made to look like a lady. He saves humans, so I've decided he isn't worth my time. Here's a picture of me instead.

White Fang. Turns out he was a wolf, not a dog, but who cares, this is my list of greatest dogs, not yours, so mind your own business. I couldn't find a photo. So here's another one of me.

POEM

Be nice to your dog
if you can

He likes to eat biscuits
and ham

Don't get a kitten

Or you'll get bitten

For cats are the work
of Satan

WHAT SHOULD YOU DO IF A CAT SPITS AT YOU?

TURN THE GRILL DOWN

WHAT DOESN'T KILL YOU

MAKES YOU GRUMPY

I THOUGHT ABOUT EMBARKING ON THE ROAD TO SUCCESS

BUT THEN I THOUGHT, WHAT'S THE POINT?

IT'S MY LIFE

AND I'LL NAP WHERE I WANT TO

I ONLY GOT UP TO SEE IF
MY LUCK HAD CHANGED

IT HADN'T

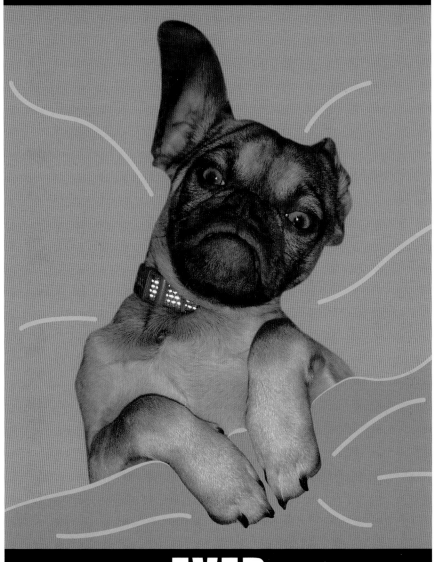

< >   X Earl

PLAYLIST
Favorite Songs
CREATED BY EARL • 5 SONGS

+ WHO LET THE DOGS OUT? (BAHA MEN)
Anthem to freedom for dogs all over the world

+ HOUND DOG (ELVIS)
The King was a dog at heart, one of us

+ BRIDGE OVER TROUBLED WATER
(SIMON AND GARFUNKEL)
I'm looking for that bridge, believe me

+ I CAN'T GET NO SATISFACTION
(ROLLING STONES)
Me neither

+ IT'S THE END OF THE WORLD
AS WE KNOW IT (REM)
Can't come soon enough, if you ask me

PLAYLIST
Stupid Songs
CREATED BY EARL • 5 SONGS

+ HAPPY (PHARRELL)
I will NEVER play this song

+ SINGIN' IN THE RAIN
Who even goes outside in the rain, let alone sings in it?
Song for idiots

+ MY FAVORITE THINGS
Raindrops on roses and whiskers on kittens?
These are my least favorite things

+ ALL YOU NEED IS LOVE (THE BEATLES)
Actually, no. All you need is peace and quiet and an
endless supply of peanut butter

+ STAIRWAY TO HEAVEN (LED ZEPPELIN)
Great. I'm not allowed on the stairs

SOMETIMES EVERYTHING SEEMS TO BE GOING SO WELL

DON'T GET EXCITED.

I SOMETIMES FEEL HAPPY

WHEN I THINK ABOUT OTHER PEOPLE'S MISFORTUNE

I WISH YOUR PARENTS

HAD NEVER MET

GOOD THINGS COME TO THOSE WHO WAIT

UNLESS YOU DIE IN THE MEANTIME

IF I KNEW WHAT I WAS GRUMPY ABOUT

I WOULD STILL BE THIS GRUMPY